I0407382

Contents

Preface

Welcome to "How to Buy Shares in Nigeria: A Comprehensive Guide." This book is designed to be your go-to resource for navigating the Nigerian stock market and making informed investment decisions. In an ever-evolving financial landscape, understanding the dynamics of stock market investing is paramount to achieving your financial goals and securing a prosperous future.

This guide is structured into ten comprehensive chapters, each aimed at providing you with the knowledge and tools necessary to confidently engage with the Nigerian stock market. We start with an introductory understanding of the stock market, progressing to fundamental financial principles, exploring the Nigerian market's historical evolution, understanding various investment strategies, and finally, equipping you with the skills to manage your portfolio effectively.

Chapter 1 introduces you to the essence of stock market investing, setting the stage for what lies ahead. Chapter 2 delves into building a strong financial foundation, ensuring you are well-prepared to navigate the investment landscape. Chapter 3 provides a detailed understanding of the Nigerian stock market, its structure, and its components.

Chapter 4 emphasizes the importance of thorough research and due diligence in making investment decisions, setting the groundwork for informed choices. Chapter 5 guides you in selecting the right stockbroker, a crucial partner in your investment journey. Chapter 6 takes you through the process of placing orders and executing trades, essential actions in the stock market.

Risk management and portfolio diversification, the focal points of Chapter 7, are pivotal aspects of securing your investments. Chapter 8 introduces you to Initial Public Offerings (IPOs) and Rights Issues, important events that can shape your investment portfolio. Investment strategies and techniques are explored in Chapter 9, providing you with a toolkit for a successful investment journey.

Lastly, Chapter 10 brings the guide full circle by detailing how to monitor and manage your investments effectively, ensuring they align with your financial objectives.

The aim is to empower you to embrace the world of stock market investments in Nigeria. I encourage continuous learning and growth, emphasizing the potential for financial prosperity through strategic investments. As you embark on this educational journey, it is my hope that you will find this guide not only informative but also inspiring, enabling you to take confident steps towards a lucrative and rewarding investment experience.

Let us navigate the world of Nigerian stock market investments together. Happy investing!

Chapter 1

Introduction to Stock Market Investing in Nigeria

Overview of the Nigerian Stock Market

The Nigerian stock market, overseen by the Nigerian Exchange (NGX) formally known as the Nigerian Stock Exchange (NSE), is a critical component of the nation's economy. It is a platform where shares, bonds, and other financial instruments are bought and sold. The NSE, established in 1960, plays a pivotal role in ensuring fair and transparent trading, providing a marketplace for companies to raise capital and investors to grow their wealth.

The Nigerian stock market is divided into various sectors representing different industries such as banking, oil and gas, consumer goods, healthcare, and more. Notable indices like the All Share Index (ASI) and market capitalization are key indicators of the overall performance of the stock market.

Importance of Investing in Shares for Financial Growth

Investing in shares is a fundamental way to grow one's wealth. When you invest in shares, you are essentially buying ownership in a company. As the company grows and prospers, the value of your shares increases, allowing you to sell them at a profit. Additionally, many companies distribute dividends, providing shareholders with a share of the company's profits.

Long-term investment in shares offers the potential for significant capital appreciation. Over time, the value of shares can multiply manifold, outpacing inflation and other traditional savings methods. This growth can lead to substantial financial gains and a more secure financial future.

Understanding the Basics of Stocks and Equities

Stocks, also known as equities or shares, represent ownership in a company. When you purchase shares, you essentially become a partial owner of that company. Shareholders participate in the company's growth and success and often have voting rights on significant company decisions.

The value of shares is influenced by various factors, including the company's performance, industry trends, economic conditions, and investor sentiment. Stock traders aim to buy shares at a lower price and sell them when the price appreciates, thus generating a profit. While some investors place their focus on dividend yield and long-term capital appreciation.

The Role of Stockbrokers and the Nigerian Exchange (NGX)

Stockbrokers act as intermediaries between investors and the stock market. They facilitate buying and selling of shares on behalf of investors, offering advice, research, and market insights. Stockbrokers also help in opening and managing brokerage accounts, providing access to trading platforms.

The Nigerian Exchange (NGX) is the primary platform where buying and selling of shares occur. It regulates and oversees the market, ensuring fair practices and maintaining market integrity. It provides an avenue for companies to list their shares, enabling them to raise capital by offering ownership stakes to the public.

Understanding the Nigerian stock market and the basics of stock investing is an initial step toward creating a prosperous financial future. By comprehending the role of shares, their potential for financial growth, and the support provided by stockbrokers and the NGX, investors can make informed decisions and embark on a rewarding investment journey in Nigeria's dynamic stock market.

Chapter 2

Building a Strong Financial Foundation

Building a strong financial foundation is essential for successful and sustainable investment ventures. It involves careful assessment of one's financial situation, setting clear goals, managing debts and expenses, and establishing a budget to pave the way for sound investment strategies. Let us look at the key steps in establishing a strong financial base.

1. Assessing Personal Financial Readiness for Investments

Assessing personal financial readiness involves evaluating one's financial position, understanding cash flow, calculating net worth, and determining risk tolerance. It is crucial to have a clear understanding of current assets, liabilities, income, and expenses. A comprehensive financial health assessment provides a realistic view of the resources available for investment.

2. Setting Clear Investment Goals and Objectives

Setting clear and achievable investment goals is fundamental. Goals should be specific, measurable, achievable, relevant, and time-bound (SMART). Whether it is buying a home, funding education, or planning for retirement, establishing well-defined objectives helps determine the investment horizon, risk tolerance, and the appropriate investment vehicles to achieve these goals.

3. Creating a Budget and Saving for Investments

Creating a budget involves tracking income and expenditures, and allocating funds for necessary expenses, savings, and investments. It is essential to prioritize saving a portion of income for investments, emergencies, and future financial goals. A disciplined approach to saving ensures a consistent stream of funds for investment opportunities.

4. Managing Debt and Credit for a Healthy Financial Foundation

Effective debt management is crucial for a strong financial foundation. This involves understanding the types of debt (e.g., mortgages, personal loans, credit card debt) and developing strategies to minimize and eliminate high-interest debt. Maintaining a good credit standing enables access to favorable interest rates and financial opportunities.

5. Strategies for Debt Management and Credit Health

a. Debt Snowball Method: Prioritize paying off smaller debts first, then redirect the funds to tackle larger debts.

b. Debt Avalanche Method: Prioritize paying off high-interest debts first to reduce the overall interest burden.

c. Regular Debt Payments: Make timely and consistent payments to maintain a good credit standing.

d. Monitoring Credit Report: Regularly review credit reports to identify errors and address discrepancies promptly.

Building a strong financial foundation is the bedrock of successful investing. Assessing financial readiness, setting clear goals, creating a budget, and effectively managing debt and credit lay the groundwork for a secure financial future. It is essential to maintain discipline, seek financial education, and consult professionals to navigate the complexities of finance and investments effectively. By following these steps, you can lay the groundwork for a robust financial base and pave the way toward achieving your financial aspirations and investment objectives.

Chapter 3

Understanding the Nigerian Stock Market

History and Evolution of the Nigerian Stock Market

The Nigerian stock market has a rich history dating back to the early 1960s. It officially began operations with the establishment of the Lagos Stock Exchange (LSE) in 1960, which later became the Nigerian Stock Exchange (NSE) in 1977. In 2021, NSE launched a new brand identity into what we know today as the Nigerian Exchange (NGX). Over the years, the market has seen significant growth, evolution, and modernization, adapting to changes in technology, regulations, and the economy.

Structure and Components of the Nigerian Stock Market

The Nigerian stock market is structured to facilitate the buying and selling of securities. Its main components include:

1. Listed Companies: These are publicly traded companies that have undergone a rigorous listing process and are allowed to trade their shares on the stock exchange.

2. Brokers and Brokerage Firms: Registered entities that facilitate the buying and selling of securities on behalf of investors.

3. Investors: Individuals, institutional investors, and foreign investors who participate in the market by buying and selling shares and other securities.

4. Regulatory Bodies: Entities responsible for regulating and overseeing the operations of the stock market, ensuring

transparency, fair trading practices, and protecting investors.

Key Indices and Sectors in the Nigerian Stock Market

The Nigerian stock market comprises various indices that track the performance of different segments of the market. Some notable indices include:

1. All Share Index (ASI): This represents the overall performance of the entire stock market, measuring the average price changes of all listed securities.

2. Sectoral Indices: Track the performance of specific sectors such as banking, consumer goods, oil and gas, industrial, and healthcare, providing insights into the health of those industries.

The Role of Regulatory Bodies like SEC and CSCS

Securities and Exchange Commission (SEC): As the apex regulatory body, SEC oversees the Nigerian capital market. It formulates rules and regulations, ensures market transparency, protects investors, and maintains the integrity and efficiency of the market.

Central Securities Clearing System (CSCS): CSCS is the clearing and settlement house for the Nigerian capital market. It provides the infrastructure for the clearing and settlement of trades, ensuring the safe and efficient transfer of securities and funds between parties.

Regulatory bodies play a crucial role in maintaining market confidence, attracting investments, and ensuring that the Nigerian stock market operates in a fair and transparent manner. Their oversight and regulatory frameworks help build trust among investors, which is essential for a thriving stock market.

Understanding the Nigerian stock market involves comprehending its historical development, structure, indices, and the role of regulatory bodies. It is an ever-evolving entity that plays a vital role in the Nigerian economy. Investors and stakeholders benefit from being informed about its workings, which aids in making sound investment decisions and contributes to the growth and stability of the nation's financial landscape.

Chapter 4

Research and Due Diligence in Stock Market Investing

Conducting Thorough Research on Potential Investments

Thorough research is the cornerstone of successful stock market investing. Before committing funds to any investment, it is vital to conduct extensive research on the company, industry, and broader market conditions. Research includes analyzing financial data, understanding the business model, studying the competitive landscape, and evaluating the company's growth prospects.

Analyzing Financial Statements and Company Performance

Analyzing a company's financial statements is a critical aspect of due diligence. Financial statements like balance sheets, income statements, and cash flow statements provide insights into a company's financial health, liquidity, debt levels, profitability, and overall performance. Ratios such as price-to-earnings (P/E), debt-to-equity, and return on equity (ROE) are valuable metrics for assessing a company's financial strength and potential for growth.

Evaluating Industry Trends and Economic Factors

Understanding industry trends and the broader economic environment is essential for making informed investment decisions. Factors like market demand, technological advancements, regulatory changes, and geopolitical events can significantly impact a company's performance and stock price. Evaluating the industry's growth potential and the company's position within it helps in determining its resilience and potential for long-term success.

Utilizing Online Resources and Financial News for Research

In the digital age, a wealth of information is available online, making it easier for investors to conduct comprehensive research. Utilize reputable financial news websites, industry reports, analyst recommendations, and company filings available on financial portals. Social media platforms, investment blogs, and forums can also provide valuable insights and discussions on potential investments.

Strategies for Effective Research and Due Diligence

1. Create a Checklist: Develop a structured checklist to ensure you cover all aspects of research for each potential investment.

2. Diversify Information Sources: Gather information from multiple reliable sources to avoid bias and get a comprehensive view of the investment opportunity.

3. Stay Updated: Regularly update your knowledge base with the latest industry news, economic indicators, and company updates to make timely investment decisions.

4. Consult Professionals: Seek advice from industry experts to gain different perspectives and validate your research findings.

Research and due diligence are paramount in mitigating investment risks and increasing the likelihood of making profitable choices. You should dedicate time and effort to thoroughly assess potential investments, considering both quantitative and qualitative factors. By staying informed, analyzing financial data, understanding market dynamics, and leveraging a variety of information sources, you can make informed decisions that align with your financial goals and risk tolerance.

Chapter 5

Selecting the Right Stockbroker

Exploring Different Types of Stockbrokers in Nigeria

Choosing the right stockbroker is a critical decision in your investment journey. In Nigeria, there are different types of stockbrokers, each with its own characteristics.

1. Full-Service Brokers: Offer a wide range of services including investment advice, research reports, portfolio management, and financial planning.

2. Discount Brokers: Provide trading services at lower commission rates but may offer limited research and advisory services.

3. Online Brokers: Facilitate trading through online platforms, giving investors the freedom to trade at their convenience. They typically have competitive commission rates.

Evaluating Brokerage Fees, Charges, and Services

Understanding the fee structure of a stockbroker is vital to managing your investment costs effectively. Consider the following factors:

1. Commission Fees: Charges for buying and selling stocks.

2. Account Maintenance Fees: Annual or periodic fees for account maintenance.

3. Transaction Charges: Fees for executing buy/sell orders.

4. Other Charges: Check for charges related to account statements, withdrawals, or transfers.

Ensure that the brokerage fees align with your investment strategy and budget.

Assessing Reputation, Reliability, and Customer Service of Brokers

A broker's reputation and reliability are paramount. Consider the following to assess a broker's credibility:

a. Track Record: Research the broker's history, years in the industry, and track record of successful transactions.

b. Client Reviews: Read reviews and testimonials from other clients to gauge customer satisfaction.

c. Regulatory Compliance: Ensure that the broker is registered with the Securities and Exchange Commission (SEC) and adheres to regulatory guidelines.

d. Customer Service: Evaluate the responsiveness and helpfulness of the broker's customer service.

Opening a Brokerage Account and Understanding the Trading Platform

Now that you have selected a broker to start with, you then proceed to opening a brokerage account. To open a brokerage account, follow these steps:

1. Documentation: Prepare the required identification and financial documents as specified by the broker.

2. Application: Complete the account application form provided by the broker.

3. Funding Your Account: Deposit the initial funds required to start trading in accordance with the instructions provided by the broker.

Understanding the trading platform is crucial. Familiarize yourself with:

- Order Placement: Learn how to place buy and sell orders through the platform.

- Market Information: Explore features providing real-time market data, charts, and analysis.

- Account Management: Understand how to track your portfolio, view account statements, and access other account-related information.

Selecting the right stockbroker is a vital step in your investment journey. Consider your investment preferences, risk tolerance, and budget when exploring different types of brokers. Evaluate their reputation, reliability, and customer service to ensure a satisfactory and trustworthy relationship. Familiarize yourself with their fee structure and the functionality of their trading platform before opening an account. Making an informed decision about your stockbroker will set a solid foundation for your successful venture into the Nigerian stock market.

You can confirm the registration of a stockbroker with SEC at; https://sec.gov.ng/cmos/

Chapter 6

Placing Orders and Executing Trades

Placing orders and executing trades are fundamental aspects of stock market participation. You need to have an in-depth understanding of the various order types, the process of executing trades through a stockbroker, comprehending trade confirmations and settlements, and effective portfolio monitoring and management.

Types of Orders: Market, Limit, Stop-Loss, and Stop-Limit

1. Market Order

A market order is a request to buy or sell a stock at the current market price. It is executed immediately at the best available price in the market.

2. Limit Order

A limit order allows you to set a specific price at which you want to buy or sell a stock. The trade will only be executed if the market price reaches or surpasses the specified limit price.

3. Stop-Loss Order

A stop-loss order is designed to protect your investments by automatically selling a stock once its price drops to a predetermined level. It helps limit potential losses.

4. Stop-Limit Order

A stop-limit order is a combination of a stop order and a limit order. When the stock hits a certain price (the stop price), a limit order is triggered, instructing the broker to buy or sell at a specific limit price.

Executing Trades through a Stockbroker

To execute trades through a stockbroker, follow these steps:

1. Account Access: Log in to your brokerage account through the trading platform provided by your broker.

2. Selecting the Stock: Choose the stock you want to buy or sell.

3. Choosing the Order Type: Decide on the type of order you want to place based on your investment strategy (market, limit, stop-loss, or stop-limit).

4. Entering Order Details: Input the stock symbol, quantity, and the price at which you want to buy or sell.

5. Review and Confirmation: Double-check the order details, review any fees associated with the trade, and confirm the trade.

Understanding Trade Confirmations and Settlements

- Trade Confirmations: After executing a trade, you will receive a confirmation detailing the specifics of the trade, including the price, quantity, transaction fees, and settlement date.

- Settlement Process: Settlement involves the exchange of funds and securities between the parties involved in the trade. The settlement period varies by market but usually takes a few days.

Monitoring and Managing Your Portfolio Effectively

a. Regular Review: Continuously monitor your portfolio's performance, ensuring it aligns with your investment goals and risk tolerance.

b. Market Analysis: Stay informed about market trends, economic developments, and industry news that may impact your investments.

c. Diversification: Maintain a diversified portfolio to spread risk across various asset classes and minimize exposure to any single asset.

d. Risk Management: Implement risk management strategies, including setting stop-loss levels and diversifying investments, to protect your portfolio from significant losses.

Placing orders and executing trades are fundamental skills for successful stock market investing. Understanding the types of orders and how to execute them, along with comprehending trade confirmations and settlements, is essential. Effective monitoring and management of your portfolio ensure that your investments remain aligned with your financial objectives. By mastering these aspects, you can navigate the stock market confidently and make informed decisions to achieve your investment goals.

Chapter 7

Risk Management and Portfolio Diversification: Safeguarding Your Investments

In the dynamic world of stock market investments, understanding and effectively managing risks is paramount to ensure the protection and growth of your portfolio. Risk management involves identifying potential risks and implementing strategies to mitigate them. Portfolio diversification, a key aspect of risk management, helps in spreading investments across various assets to achieve a balance between risk and return.

Identifying Different Types of Risks in Stock Market Investments

1. Market Risk: Arises due to market fluctuations affecting the overall value of investments.

2. Company Risk: Specific to the company whose stock you own, encompassing management issues, financial health, and market position.

3. Liquidity Risk: The risk of not being able to buy or sell an investment quickly at a fair price due to insufficient market liquidity.

4. Interest Rate Risk: The risk that changes in interest rates will affect investment values, especially in bonds.

5. Inflation Risk: The loss of purchasing power of money over time due to rising prices.

Strategies to Mitigate Risks and Protect Investments

1. Asset Allocation: Spread investments across diverse asset classes (e.g., stocks, bonds, real estate) to minimize exposure to any single type of risk.

2. Stop-Loss Orders: Implement stop-loss orders to automatically sell a security when its price falls to a certain level, limiting potential losses.

3. Research and Due Diligence: Thoroughly research investments before making decisions, analyzing company fundamentals, industry trends, and economic indicators.

4. Regular Portfolio Review: Continuously monitor your portfolio's performance and make adjustments to align with your risk tolerance and financial goals.

Importance of Diversification for a Resilient Portfolio

Diversification is key to managing risk effectively. By diversifying your investments, you spread risk across various assets, thereby reducing the impact of negative performance in any single investment. A diversified portfolio can potentially provide more stable returns over time and withstand market volatility.

Balancing Risk and Return in Your Investment Strategy

Balancing risk and return involves finding the optimal trade-off between potential gains and the level of risk you are willing to tolerate. Higher-risk investments often come with the potential for higher returns, but they also pose a greater risk of losses. Consider your financial goals, risk tolerance, and investment horizon when formulating an investment strategy to strike the right balance.

Understanding and managing risks is fundamental to successful investing. By identifying different types of risks and implementing appropriate strategies to mitigate them, you can safeguard your investments. Portfolio diversification is a crucial tool in managing risk, providing resilience against market fluctuations. Balancing risk and return is essential to create an investment strategy that aligns with your financial objectives. Continuously educate yourself, stay informed, and adjust your strategies to effectively manage risk and achieve your long-term investment goals.

Chapter 8

Initial Public Offerings (IPOs) and Rights Issues

IPOs and their Significance in the Stock Market

An Initial Public Offering (IPO) is the first time a private company offers its shares to the public for purchase, thereby becoming a publicly traded entity. This process involves transitioning from private ownership to a public one, where ownership stakes are sold to external investors, including institutional and retail traders. The significance of an IPO lies in its capacity to provide the company with significant capital for expansion, debt reduction, or other business objectives. Additionally, IPOs increase the company's visibility and credibility in the financial market.

Participating in an IPO and Understanding the IPO Process

Participating in an IPO requires investors to purchase shares through brokerage firms involved in the IPO process. The IPO process typically involves the following steps:

1. Preparation and Due Diligence: The company and underwriters assess the business, determine the offering price, and prepare the necessary documentation.

2. Filing and Regulatory Approval: The Company files a registration statement with the regulator, the SEC, outlining essential information about the company.

3. Roadshow and Marketing: Company representatives and underwriters conduct roadshows to present the

investment opportunity to potential investors, explaining the company's prospects and financials.

4. Pricing and Allotment: The final IPO price is determined based on investor interest during the roadshow. Shares are allocated to investors based on demand and other factors.

5. Listing and Trading: The shares are then listed on a stock exchange, and trading begins.

Engaging in Rights Issues and Subscription Rights

Rights issues allow existing shareholders to purchase additional shares at a discounted price, usually in proportion to their existing holdings. This can be a way for a company to raise capital from its current shareholders. Shareholders receive subscription rights, granting them the opportunity to purchase these new shares during a specified subscription period.

Opportunities and Risks Associated with IPOs and Rights Issues

Opportunities:

1. Potential for High Returns: IPOs can offer significant returns if the company performs well post-listing, especially if it becomes a market leader or experiences rapid growth.

2. Early Investment in Promising Companies: Participating in an IPO enables investors to become early stakeholders in a potentially successful venture, possibly benefiting from long-term capital appreciation.

3. Liquidity and Market Visibility: IPOs provide liquidity and market exposure, making it easier for a company to raise capital in the future and facilitate acquisitions.

Risks:

1. Market Volatility: IPOs can experience significant price fluctuations initially, and the market's reception may not meet expectations.

2. Lack of Historical Data: Limited historical data makes it challenging to accurately evaluate the company's performance and future potential.

3. Underperformance: The Company may not meet revenue or growth projections, resulting in a decline in the stock's value and disappointing returns for investors.

In summary, both IPOs and rights issues are fundamental mechanisms for companies to raise capital and for investors to participate in potential growth. However, they carry inherent risks, requiring investors to conduct thorough due diligence and consider their risk tolerance before engaging in either.

Chapter 9

Investment Strategies and Techniques

Long-term Investing vs. Short-term Trading: Pros and Cons

Long-term Investing
Long-term investing involves buying and holding investments for an extended period, often years or even decades.

Pros:
1. Potential for Higher Returns: Historically, long-term investments tend to yield higher returns due to the compounding effect.
2. Lower Transaction Costs: Fewer transactions mean lower fees and taxes.
3. Reduced Market Volatility Impact: Long-term investors are less affected by short-term market fluctuations.

Cons:
1. Lack of Liquidity: Assets may not be easily converted to cash without potential loss.
2. Patience Required: It demands discipline and a long-term perspective, which not all investors may have.

Short-term Trading
Short-term trading involves buying and selling assets within a shorter time frame, often within a day or a few weeks.

Pros:
1. Quick Profits: It provides opportunities to capitalize on short-term market movements for immediate gains.
2. Flexibility: Traders can adapt to changing market conditions and adjust their strategies accordingly.

Cons:
1. Higher Transaction Costs: Frequent trades result in higher transaction fees and taxes.
2. Greater Market Volatility Exposure: Short-term trading is more susceptible to market volatility and unpredictable price swings.

Value Investing, Growth Investing, and Income Investing

Value Investing:
Value investing involves identifying undervalued stocks or assets based on fundamental analysis, aiming to buy at a lower price than their intrinsic value.

Growth Investing:
Growth investing focuses on investing in companies with high growth potential, even if the current valuation may seem relatively high, based on expectations of future earnings and revenue growth.

Income Investing:
Income investing prioritizes investments that generate regular income, such as dividends from stocks, interest from bonds, or rental income from real estate.

Technical Analysis and Charting for Investment Decisions

Technical analysis involves studying past market data, primarily price and volume, to forecast future price movements. Charting is a key component, using visual representations like candlestick charts and trend lines to analyze historical patterns.

Pros:
1. Short-term Insights: It will help you to identify short-term trends and trading opportunities.
2. Visualization of Data: The charts provide a visual representation of market behavior.

Cons:
1. Limited Fundamental Data: Technical analysis may not consider fundamental aspects like a company's financials or broader economic factors.
2. Subjectivity: Interpretation of charts can vary among analysts, leading to potential discrepancies in conclusions.

Building a Diversified Investment Portfolio for Steady Growth

A diversified portfolio may include a mix of stocks, bonds, real estate, commodities, and cash.

Benefits:
a. Risk Mitigation: Diversification helps spread risk across different assets, reducing the impact of a decline in any single investment.
b. Potential for Steady Growth: Different assets may perform well at different times, it therefore provides a steadier overall portfolio growth.

Considerations:
a. Asset Allocation: Allocate investments based on risk tolerance, financial goals, and investment horizon.
b. Regular Review: Rebalance the portfolio periodically to maintain the desired asset allocation as market conditions and goals change.

Choosing the right investment strategy and technique depends on an investor's risk tolerance, financial goals, and time horizon. A balanced approach considering both short-term trading and long-term investing, along with a diversified portfolio, can help achieve steady growth while managing risk.

Chapter 10

Monitoring Your Investments and Future Growth

Setting up a Systematic Monitoring System for Your Portfolio

Establishing a systematic monitoring system for your portfolio is crucial for ensuring that your investments align with your financial goals. Here is how to do it:

1. Regular Tracking: Monitor your investments on a consistent basis, whether it is daily, weekly, or monthly, to stay informed about their performance.

2. Utilize Technology: Leverage investment tracking apps, portfolio management software, or online platforms to conveniently track your portfolio's value, asset allocation, and transactions.

3. Document Transactions: Maintain a detailed record of all your transactions, including purchase/sale dates, quantities, prices, and any associated fees or taxes.

Analyzing Performance and Making Informed Decisions

Effective analysis of your portfolio's performance is vital for making informed decisions that can impact your future growth

1. Performance Metrics: Utilize various metrics like Return on Investment (ROI), Sharpe ratio, standard deviation, and alpha to evaluate the performance of individual assets and the portfolio as a whole.

2. Benchmarking: Compare your portfolio's performance against relevant market benchmarks to gauge how well your investments are doing compared to the broader market.

3. Risk Assessment: Assess the level of risk associated with your investments and evaluate if it aligns with your risk tolerance and long-term objectives.

Rebalancing Your Portfolio and Adjusting Investment Strategies

Regularly rebalancing your portfolio ensures that your investment strategy remains aligned with your financial goals and risk tolerance:

a. Asset Allocation Review: Periodically review your asset allocation to ensure it still matches your investment goals. Adjust allocations based on changing financial needs, risk tolerance, and market conditions.

b. Reinvestment Strategy: Reinvest dividends, interest, or any profits earned to maintain your target asset allocation or acquire new assets in line with your investment strategy.

Planning for the Future and Evolving as an Informed Investor

As an informed investor, you have to plan for your future growth and adapt to changing circumstances.

1. Goal Reassessment: Regularly review and reassess your financial goals, adjusting your investment strategies and contributions accordingly.

2. Continuous Learning: Stay updated on financial markets, investment trends, and new opportunities. Consider reading financial literature, attending seminars, or consulting with industry experts.

3. Tax Efficiency: Explore tax-saving investment options to maximize your after-tax returns. Do your best to understand the tax implications for different investment types.

4. Emergency Preparedness: Ensure that you have an emergency fund and appropriate insurance coverage to protect your investments from unexpected financial setbacks.

A systematic approach to monitoring your investments, analyzing performance, rebalancing your portfolio, and planning for the future is essential for sustainable and informed investment growth. Regularly review your investments, stay informed about market trends, and evolve your strategies to align with your financial aspirations.

Conclusion

The world of stock market investing offers a promising avenue for achieving financial prosperity, and the potential for growth is particularly significant in Nigeria. However, to truly harness this potential, it is imperative to cultivate a mindset of continuous learning and growth in the realm of investments.

Investing in the stock market is not a one-time affair. It is a journey of constant evolution and learning. With the dynamic nature of financial markets, staying informed about the latest trends, investment strategies, and economic changes is paramount. Regularly updating one's knowledge through reputable sources, seeking advice from industry experts, and learning from experiences, both successes and failures, are crucial to making informed and sound investment decisions.

Nigeria, with its growing economy and vibrant financial markets, presents an abundance of investment opportunities. Strategic investments in sectors like technology, agriculture, energy, and consumer goods can potentially yield substantial returns. By conducting thorough research, understanding the local market dynamics, and aligning investments with long-term financial objectives, investors can unlock the vast potential for financial growth and prosperity.

The world of finance is ever-evolving, influenced by global economic shifts, policy changes, and technological advancements. Staying updated with these changes is crucial to adapt and optimize investment strategies. Being aware of market trends, regulatory alterations, and emerging industries enables investors to pivot and position their portfolios for maximum growth while mitigating risks.

It is with great enthusiasm and inspiration that I encourage you to take your first steps into the world of stock market investments in Nigeria. Start by setting clear financial goals, understanding your risk tolerance, and developing a diversified investment portfolio. Seek guidance from industry experts or mentors, utilize reliable investment platforms, and embark on this journey with prudence and determination.

In conclusion, the realm of stock market investments holds immense potential for financial growth and prosperity, and with informed decisions, continuous learning, and a strategic approach, individuals can shape a secure and prosperous financial future for themselves and their families. Take those first crucial steps towards a future of financial abundance in the Nigerian stock market. Best wishes!